City Shapes
and other Poems

Contents

City Shapes	2
Flags	6
Seaside Street	8
Rain Clouds	10
Skyscrapers	12
Kite	14

Poems by Alan Durant

Illustrated by Rachael Saunders

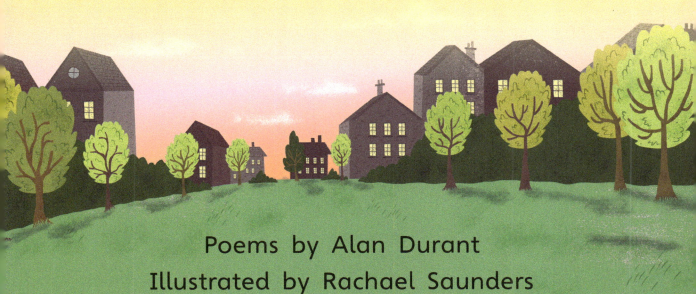

City Shapes

The sun wakes up.
It's a brand new day!
The sun shines on the city
And the darkness fades away.

The sun shines its light
On the high roof tops,
On a clock tower, a bridge,
A palace, houses, shops.

There are shapes in the city.
You can see them everywhere:
Triangles and circles,
Rectangles and squares.

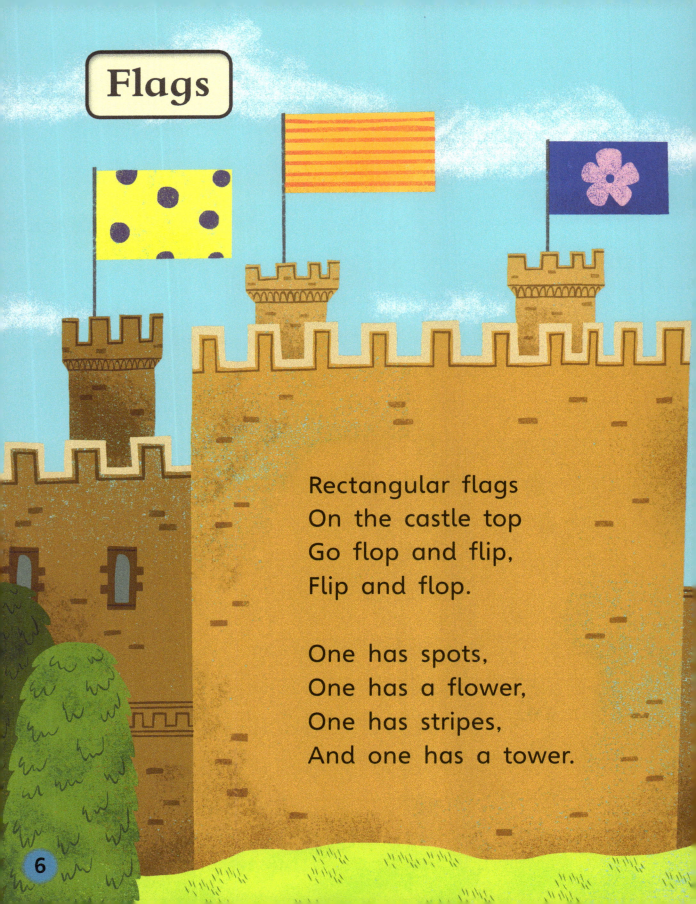

Flags

Rectangular flags
On the castle top
Go flop and flip,
Flip and flop.

One has spots,
One has a flower,
One has stripes,
And one has a tower.

This flag is red,
This flag is green,
This flag has a crown
Like a king or queen.

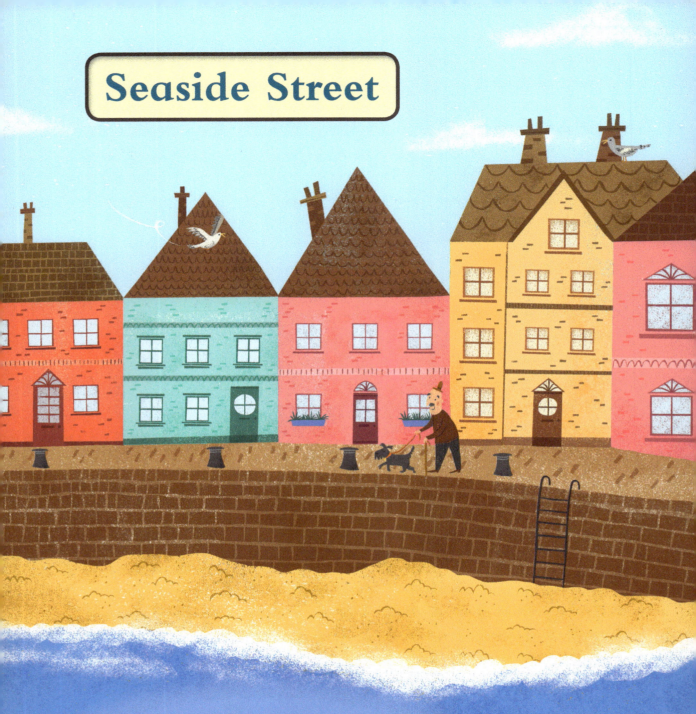

Seaside Street

Houses are squares
With triangles on their heads.
All in a neat row
Yellows, greens and reds.

The windows are squares,
That people can look through.
Can you see the boy?
He's waving down at you!

Rain Clouds

The stormy clouds are black
Above the round, green hills.
They open up like sacks
And down the cold rain spills!

Skyscrapers

Tall, thin towers
Stand huge and high
Like blocks of icy silver
In the bright blue sky.

Some windows are triangles.
Some doors go round and round.
Skyscrapers' heads are in the clouds,
Their feet are in the ground.

Kite

The white kite
Flies up high,
Like a diamond
In the sky.

Away it floats
Like a balloon,
Over the houses
Up to the moon.

Good night, kite.
Good night, moon.
Good night, sky.
See you soon!